# The Prince
# And
# The Four Gardens

## Rev. David E. Clarke

Rev. David E. Clarke
P.O. 82
Ashville, Ohio 43103

Published by FWB Publications
Columbus, Ohio

**FWB**

**Rev. David E. Clarke**

## DEDICATION

To those who did
To those who did not
To those who should
To those who should not
To those who stayed
To those who stayed not
To those who loved
To those who loved not

To He who did all and does all and will do all,

Ho Kurios Mou Kai Ho Theos Mou

## ACKNOWLEDGEMENTS

I would like to give my thanks and appreciation to the many people in my life who have touched me and helped me.

I would thank Mr. Timothy Perkins for his friendship and support over the many years he has been my friend and source of support.

I extend my thanks to the churches I have been in fellowship during my journey in the Lord.

Thanks go to my family who I love.

My many thanks are extended to my publisher and friend, Dr. Alton Loveless.

# PREFACE

This parable was first published in my earlier work, *"Concerning the Christ."*

I felt that it may be accepted as a work on its own. My hope and my desire is to glorify my Lord and Savior, the Lord Jesus Christ. The goal of this short work is to accomplish that goal to some degree as it is within me to do.

The liberties I have taken within this work were taken to facilitate the telling of the great story within a short framework.

# THE PRINCE
# AND
# THE FOUR GARDENS

*A PARABLE*

Once there was a prince who was
the son of the king who ruled a vast
land.  His kingdom stretched from one
edge of the horizon to the other.  The
king was a just and righteous ruler.  His
son was good and obedient.  There was
peace and contentment in all the land
save one tiny particular valley.

The sun rose on the dawn of the day
and the king knew it was time.  Time to
remedy the ills of discontentment
found within the valley.  The king had
sent first one emissary and then
another to regain and restore peace in
this troublesome vale.  The folk were
contrary disregarding and rejecting the
representatives the king had sent.  The
folk within the dale of the king's
kingdom accepted no plan from the

ruler. The king knew that he must send someone more than a mere ambassador. The king decided to send his son, the good and obedient prince.

The prince arose and began his journey. In the fullness of time and after many days of travel, the son topped a rugged hill and looked over the landscape of the valley of the rebellious subjects. He turned his head looking first this way and then the other. He looked down the hill's side, over the basin and up the other side of the neighboring hill that formed the valley. The prince knew that the peace and future of this place rested upon him. He began his descent into the vale.

The journey down the hill, while arduous, seemed to go quickly enough. Soon the prince came upon a garden. This garden had seen its better days. It was in disarray. The tract exuded the discard and disruption of misuse and corruption. The plot was old and had lived for a long time. Apparent to the viewing, it had suffered the burden of neglect and lack of attention from its gardener. From the thistles, thorns grew the size of a man's thumb. Weeds like bushes grew where once there had been a crop's bounty. With sadness, the prince lowered his head and sighed an audible sigh. Neglect and misuse made his heart heavy with concern, worry and pity.

In a bit of time, the prince looked about this troubled place and his eyes fell to an out of the ordinary picture. An unusual looking little man sat in the shade of an unkempt little shrub of a tree. He was odd in that he looked as neglected and tattered as the garden. He was as unkempt in appearance as the trees and bushes around him. One casual look into his eyes and one knew the odd man's unhappiness and even meanness he held within his heart. The slight man looked up and a sneer replaced the blank look that had been on his face. He looked upon the prince and stood and threw out his chest and raised his chin with an air of superiority and pride. He strolled past the thorns and thistly weeds of the patch and came close near the prince.

"Why are you in my garden," bellowed the man with a scorn and vileness in his voice?" "You'll upset my handiwork. My toil and trouble will fall to nothing. Leave my garden be as I have spent much time doing my life's work here in this place. Why are you here," questioned the odd keeper of the neglected plot?

The prince looked him full in the eyes and said, "Your garden? When did this become your garden? Your work here is of a kind that lends itself to no good thing. It is the sort of work that is destructive and not constructive. Destroying and not good."

The man recoiled from the accusation, but soon recovered and hollered at the prince, "This is my garden! I own it. I do. I bought it from the owner. He may have received it years back from someone else, but he sold it to me! I have a deed," the man bellowed while patting himself from one pocket to another as if to find it. The man, failing to find the deed still rose up with a self-important pride and continued, "The king may think he can send you here like those others," he snarled. "Those ambassadors and such who came here before. They came to me, but this is my place, my garden, my valley now. I have and own the deed to it. I would show it to you if I could but find it. It is all mine!"

The mean retort of the odd diminutive man seemed not to deter or take aback the prince. He calmly replied, "It was not anyone's to sell. It belonged and still remains the property of my father, the king.

"Ah, so you are the prince, the son of the king, mmmm," snorted the man? I have heard of you. I have even known that someday you would come here, but you have no business here regardless. Like I said before, others have come, but they also had no business here. This is my garden, my property. I might suggest in my kindness," as the sarcastic and caustic words flowed from his lips, "that you leave here before some serious kind of trouble might arise!"

The prince looked about the garden with all its neglect and at the odd man with his angry, mean and arrogant air and replied, "Though this is my father's vale. Though this is my father's realm, I will buy this plot from you. I will pay the price for the deed of ownership. My father many years ago gave this garden and this entire valley to certain folk. They owned it before you were around to neglect this garden. They should not have sold it to you or anyone else. It was not theirs to sell though my father gave it to them. He was still the king of the kingdom. They were mistaken or had to be misled in some manner. They must have sold it to you by way of deception. We both know that you deceived them. Don't we? We both know for you to own this garden you must have told them a lie. Perhaps you promised them a promise you could not nor would be willing to keep. Now little man what is your price? How much to sell this corrupt neglected plot of land back to me? To sell it back to my father who has sent me though he is the original owner?"

"Mmmm," the man uttered aloud as he thought to himself what to do. This matter required thought and reason. He must deal with the prince differently than the previous ambassadors who were sent from the king. "I must make the price so very high that the prince wouldn't value the land anymore," thought the evil gardener to himself. He believed the prince was like he was; limited in his concern and care. There had to be a price the prince would not be willing to pay. A fee so unimaginable to this son of a king. "Mmmm," he heard himself say again and replied to the prince, "Why let me think a moment," as he stroked his beard attempting to look his most cerebral and thoughtful. He had a thought. A thought that made his voice rise with glee at his own wit. "Why I believe that a fair price for this garden would be all that you have. All that you are. Prince of the land if you want this garden back that is my price. That is the fee I insist of you."

The good and obedient prince, without a lapse and without a moment of time going by announced to the bizarre creature who reveled in his wit and self-importance, "Sold!"

The unkempt gardener's eyes went large. His mouth flew open in surprise and shock at the reply to his offer. The response and readiness of the prince shocked the man and caused him to reel in his stance. Reality finally set in and the man could only hang his head in resignation. He knew that the prince was serious. He knew that the prince had accepted the offer and would pay the unspeakable price demanded. His victory in retaining the corrupt garden would be achieved only by the reluctance and rejection of his price by the prince. The improbable had not even crossed his mind. If the prince would pay the price of all that he was and had, the odd garden keeper would fail in his task. The garden would return to the king's rightful possession. The garden would be redeemed.

The prince repeated in a louder voice, "Sold!" The prince without a second look turned from the peculiar small keeper of the fraudulent garden and strolled away going deeper into the valley of rebellion.

The little man could only follow. He felt deep inside of his being a loss, a failure. This day had just begun and who could know what the remainder might bring. He could only follow the prince. He had to know what else, what other plans the prince had in store. This was his valley. All of it. Well, until today. Until today this had been a perfect little garden within a perfect little valley place for this odd little man.

Soon the son of the king came upon a second garden with the out of the ordinary tiny gardener close in tow. The prince looked all about him. This second patch was a garden of wilderness. A garden so wild, overgrown and desolate in its very appearance it bespoke an evil present in a most foreboding sense. The dutiful son continued to look about this new garden. His eyes came upon a stump of a tree and he crossed the distance and sat down upon the stump to continue looking over the wilderness garden.

His attention was interrupted by the strange man speaking, "I own this garden also. I am so, so proud of my work here." He smirked a smirk and continued his prate, "I know you have chosen to buy back the first garden with your very being. A price I cannot believe you are willing to pay. Before you say anything let me offer you this patch in addition. It is a garden of potential and promise. Look! This garden can be used for food," he coaxed as he brushed back a shrub as if it were an apple tree. I know you see wasteland perhaps, but it is fertile here and will grow anything you could desire." He stooped down and grabbed a handful of the neglected dirt and held it up and toward the prince as if to make his point. As if he was attempting to tempt the young man.

"Perhaps you are not hungry. Well, mmmm let's see. You could use this ground for power. Look at the influence you could muster with others here in the valley by owning this plot. No one else could boast of it. Just you and you alone. Everyone will know you have authority if you control this wasteland; oh sorry I meant this garden," spoke the gardener in his most sincere voice.

"You are the king's son. You know nothing can befall you. You are under the king's protection. A person would have to be crazy to trouble you. You can do what you wish. Your father has given you that right, hasn't he? Maybe you have thought that you might like to control something in your own name. Mmmm, is that right? Your very own name. Not as a prince, but as the king. The king of your own garden. You can have this garden for it is under my ownership and control. I will ask such a small price for this plot that in return will give you the greatest provision, power and position of anyone in the whole of the valley. Think of it, the whole of the valley. What will you offer me for this land? You have offered yourself for the first, what for the second?"

The prince looked at the troll of a man and replied, "Well, what is the price? The price for this wilderness garden you might wish to exact from me in order to redeem it back to my father, the king? I seek no land of my own. No power of my own. I do the work of my father, the king. So what is your price for the redemption of this plot of wilderness?"

Again the gardener stroked his beard as he had in the first garden. When he raised his eyebrows in a shrewdly manner, he said, "I am not the king's son. I am not a prince. If you acknowledge me as the original owner of this garden, mmmm the one with rule. The one in charge right here and now it can all be yours," spewing out the words in a vehemence and anger and pointing his boney gnarled finger toward the ground of the garden. He swept both his arms all around as if demonstrating an epic view for all to see. "All yours, O prince. Do you hear me?" He struck his most self-impressive stance and thrust out his chest and lifted his face and continued, "It is a small thing for you to do. Just this one small thing." Then he added with a chuckle in his voice, "And this garden with its food and fortune and fame will be yours for the taking!"

The prince appeared for a second to recoil in distaste and disgust at this very suggestion. To give the king's power and authority away only for a second to this odd creature would be incomprehensible to the obedient son. With a calmness that another would be unable to muster given the situation, the prince replied, "O little man, you think yourself smart and wise. You know so little. You act and bluster about like you are the end all of all things. Let me tell you something you may not, but should have already known. You've been around for a while. You should be aware of this fact. My father, as in the case of the first garden owns this plot as well. From the beginning, it was his and his alone. You brag and prance and smirk in your arrogance, but none of this is yours. You stole this garden of wilderness by deceit and chicanery as you seized the garden of corruption. Don't you know that my father provides. My father is the power. My father gives and takes and allows all their position in life. He is the king. It is not yours in any manner to give these things away, but his. I think this plot will again come under the control of my father both in fact and practice. It will be restored as a garden of the king. This wilderness doesn't scare or concern me. I know this is merely a reflection of you and your deceitful lies. I have agreed to the price of the first garden. That same price is sufficient also for this second plot of land. I will take this wasteland for it has been under your oversight for too long and is also my father's. I am his right arm here in this valley. Leave me! You annoy me with your simper and foolishness!"

The little man's boast and bragging gave way to a fear. A real fear he felt in his confrontation with the prince. The prince's truth smashed over the gardener's lie. He threw up his hands as if to block a given blow from the prince. The blow was in actuality to his sense of reality. It was not of hands or fists, but the words of truth the gardener heard and what he saw in the royal eyes of the prince's anger and strong resolve. The purpose of the son stood higher than his purpose of deception. He dipped his face behind his cloak as if to block this blow of truth and turned to leave the good prince. He heard the prince's words ring again in his ears as he scurried away, "What I will pay for the first I will also give as the price for this garden. O foolish little man, leave me!"

The tiny man's fear compelled him to leave the presence of the prince. With the man gone, the prince felt a peace around and through him. It was like a shower of rain that refreshes all around. The prince knew that the second garden was still a wilderness. He knew that the first garden of deceit along with this one would still require a payment, but for a time he had peace. A peace that was present before the coming conflict. The calm before the conflict. The inevitable conflict. The prince rested.

He raised his head and looked about the garden. In the distance, he saw another garden. Though he felt peace with his decision to pay the first and second gardens' price of redemption, he knew his journey must continue. He rose from the stump where he had been sitting. He decided to visit the new field. Perhaps he would continue his rest there, but the trip had to continue. He knew that He must complete his father's business.

He looked up and toward the setting sun. Night was coming. The ebony of the dark was falling like a curtain shading away the light of the sun.

The prince traveled and came to the third garden. His trek was made the easier and quicker with the pondering of the day's events. He thought of the odd little arrogant man and the two beds he had seen. A plot constructed upon lies and deceit and whose crop was the same. A second one corrupted by wilderness. He shuddered a bit considering the evil he had felt exuding from the gardener. "The curse of this entire valley originates from him," thought the prince. A curse, dark and foreboding and a harbinger of the result that arises from lies and neglect.

He stood before the entrance to the third garden. His feelings and reflections of the two previous fields, the odd man and the prince's future obligations to liberate this cursed valley laid heavily on his mind. The garden of a burden would give no rest this night to the good and dutiful prince. It was in this valley the prince felt the burden of his task.

Deference to his father was the only option for the prince. His father was the king of this garden. In fact, he was the king of all gardens and hills and all valleys from here to there. This place of burden required also to come under the rule and sovereignty of the king.

Like the two previous gardens, this garden needed in kind to be purchased. There was only one price by the payer of the price, the one that did the king's business, the prince. The price of the two gardens was he, himself. The prince knew that it was the ultimate price and would be sufficient for one garden or two or three or the entire valley. His sacrifice would cover the redemptive cost to secure the purchase. His burden was not made the easier with the knowledge. He was weighed down with heavy thoughts of the fee which would be necessary. He was tossed in his mind by the heavy winds of burden and concern. Long was the night in the prince's difficult turmoil.

The day arose and the long night came to an end. With the rising sun a peace came again to the son, the prince. He had accepted with willingness the task necessary to fulfill the king's plan. With his obedience, the plan of the king would find its inevitable success. The prince knew and had always known that he was to be the method of restoration for the entire valley. Though grueling and tasking, the travail would be accomplished. Knowing this gave the prince a peace of mind that outweighed the burden of the night.

He stood from where he had been resting and turned to walk his path. The gardens of deceit and wilderness and burden had been walked through and experienced. He had offered himself as the price of the first two gardens. He knew that the third garden would require the same price. He continued to check about. He knew that that odd little man would make his appearance. The prince found it amazing that this gardener thought himself to be in charge someway. "What a sorry delusion," thought the prince. "What a pitiful case."

The sun was shining high and darkness was well removed as the day moved along its usual course. The prince shook himself from a sudden chill he felt. He turned right and then left looking this and then that way up the pathway. He began to hear noises and sounds as he looked along the path and then saw the origin. The peculiar slight man from the gardens was there and had come with a crowd of people. "A crowd," thought the prince to himself, "Perhaps a mob was a more accurate description." One could fill the intensity and anger coming from the grouping. They seemed so adamant in their purpose.

The prince heard the gardener yell, "Now prince, now! The time is now!" The mob yelled and screamed in agreement with the bellowing of the man. "Now," the man repeated.

"Now," agreed the crowd!

"You owe me my price for those two gardens," he cackled and chuckled in his ecstasy and glee.

Accosted by the rant of the man and the accompanying crowd, the good prince announced, "I have a third garden also. For you see, I have been to the garden of the burden. I have spent the long night through and have seen the sun rise. I will own this garden of burden along with the first two." He spoke with a serenity that was a great contrast to the manic and chaos of the crowd. The prince raised his right hand and swept the vista from the first garden to the second and then the third. In triumph, he spoke, "I know it is time for me to pay the price. I am willing!" As he spoke, a stillness of both manner and spirit came from him that stopped the din of the crowd. They all fell silent as they stood watching and listening to the few words that had just been spoken. The son of the king continued, "In fact, I am going to not only buy the fields, but this entire valley. All of it! No more will anyone live in these hard gardens that you have ravaged with your hate and evil. You have meant this valley and these gardens to be a mean task for these people though they may not perceive it. I will use this labor that is required to free them and to bring them back under the king, my father. This valley is not meant to be one of despair and pain, but a place of peace and contentment in service to the king. The price you have required is sufficient. It is sufficient for the first, the second and the third gardens. It is sufficient for the entire valley you think you own. I am heir to all. I am sufficient for the price."

The peculiar gardener rose to his greatest height. The crowd about him also seemed to rise at his cue. Suddenly in one voice and in a harmony of angry discord, they sang a chant of their purpose. "Now! Now!" In one motion and moment like an ocean wave, they rushed the good prince. Screaming their mantra, "Now!" over and over again, their voices rising in a giddiness of violence, they stormed the good and obedient son. All of them being led by the peculiar man were in agreement in their chore of rebellion.

"We will have no one over us," a person cried from the crowd and was repeated by others.

"This is our valley. Why do you come here? We don't want you!"

The prince lowered his head a bit not in defeat but in concern and worry as the crowd leaped upon him. Even amid the chaotic din of the crowd, the prince was heard to softly say, "I will pay the price."

In their violence and crime, the crowd egged on by the gardener beat and bloodied the prince. All agreeing, they tore at him. They pummeled him with fist and foot. They cried in their lust and lack of inhibition in a common voice both outrageous and insane. They all might have thought that they had a victory over the son. They did not understand the depth of the event. They did not see the scope of the deed being played out by the prince.

They may have considered what was occurring to be their plan, but they were wrong. The plan was not the crowds who fell under the delusion of the little man.

The little man in like kind may have thought he was victorious in his wants and plans for the valley, but he was wrong. The plan was not the gardener's wishing to keep something that was not his. It was not his plan, but his undoing.

The plan was the son's and his father's. The method of payment. The act of redemption for the entire valley.

The deed was complete now. The

good son lay among them dead and lifeless. At the man's bidding and urging, the crowd had done away with the excellent dutiful son of the king.

In their revelry of supposed victory, the mass grabbed hold of the fallen son and started to carry him up the pathway. They headed for the small valley town in which they lived. Led by the odd man, the throng with their cargo began singing and hooting in loud voices their victory over a rule they did not wish. They thought to a man surely, the king's plan had met with failure. "Who else could come to them? Who else could try to take their independence and freedom from them after the prince's death? Surely, no one would try again," they all thought. Their collective chests puffed out. There was a swagger of self-pride from each person in the convoy as it went toward the town.

The throng walked a final curve in the path and topped the final hill entering their town. They carried the prince to the center of the town to their cemetery. It was decided that there, in the middle of the town square, they would bury the prince as a type of trophy for all to see. "The tomb had to be the end of everything against them," thought the crowd. "Death was the end of everything. Surely!" They laid the prince in a squared marble tomb. Several of the mob closed the gate to the tomb. All felt secure in their delusion. All felt gleeful in ignorance and self-importance.

The prince was dead. The little gardener pranced about with a superiority and victory he had never known before. The crowd slapped one and another on their backs. They thanked the little man for his wise counsel and advice. Without the odd man, the crowd knew that they would not have known the prince was even in their valley. "We have been saved by the gardener for sure," cried out the crowd.

The prince was dead and buried. The deed was done. The odd little man snorted and snickered at his own clever wit. The prince paid the price, but the object of the payment could not be demanded if the prince was dead. The prince was gone and the gardener snickered once more, "I still have the valley! I still have all of them. All of the people." If the mob had been a bit less ecstatic and more aware, they could have heard him say, "I have won! I have won! They are mine and mine they will remain! Surely!"

The day came and went and
darkness settled over the tomb and the
town. The townspeople continued in
their revelry and celebration. They
declared a holiday in honor of their
success.

The tomb lay quiet and sealed. The
day passed.

Another night came and went and a
second sun rose. Day came to the town
in the valley. The festivities had started
to quiet and wane. The holiday had
settled into a macabre realization of the
gravity of their deed.

Some of the townspeople started to
murmur of how they had been
rash. "Oh," they said in quiet whispers
to others who replied in quiet
whispers, "Oh, we know that we had to
do it, but what if the prince was not our
doom, but our salvation? What have

we done?"

Others would just mumble a cryptic reply. Some others agreed, but were quick to add that the deed was done and that was that. The day came and went. The sun started to ebb and give way to the moon. A second day had passed. The tomb was quiet.

The third day came and a rumbling came from the earth. The sound grew in intensity and soon filled the ears of the people in the town. The din rose to such a level it appeared the rumble's clamor could be heard throughout the entire valley. The noise's center came from the sepulcher of the prince. Townspeople emerged from their homes. The clatter called them as a beacon might on a stormy sea. Some folk had a look of amazement and others a look of distress. A few broached the idea of the rightness or wrongness of their deed; a look of worry and regret. But all were looking toward the tomb; the origin of the rumbling. What was the noise? What was the cause of their alarm and worry? All knew there was cause for concern and fret. No coincidence could account for the earth shaking in the town's square. Still the folk continued to make their way to the square. They were drawn as a moth to a fire's flame of light.

All knew something different has happening. Their revelry, license and abandon of the last two days changed into a heavy weight upon their hearts. Guilt and contrition began to rise within the townsfolk and began to consume all present.

The evil odd little gardener came from an alley between two small houses near the town square to view what was going on. He had felt the disturbance. He had heard the din of the rumble. He had to preserve his victory. He gazed upon the faces of the valley folk and knew that something was wrong with both his plan and his once deluded followers.

The ground began to shake with a greater fierceness. The alarm could be sensed in the very air and the folk breathed in deeply their anxiety. The noise grew from under the ground and a small quake broke about the square. Rocks and trees moved to the motion of the force of the disturbance. The people started to panic. The little man started to recoil for within himself he had started to know the truth he once had desired to hide.

The tremor came from the square and moved through the town to the far edges of the valley. All in the valley saw the sight. All sensed they needed to come toward the town. Soon all the ground and trees within the entire valley shook with a disturbance that no one, no thing to this degree had felt before.

In an interim that seemed to go on for a long, long time, most of the people of the valley had made their way to the town's square. At the height of the quake and when all seemed lost and their concern was the greatest, a light of purest white came from the tomb. Came was not the correct word. The light burst from the tomb as explosive as a blast. The town's folk turned their faces from the light so great was its brightness.

Even the strange man turned his face. No one could stand the white light for very long. It was too penetrating.

Suddenly, in front of the crowd and before the peculiar little man of deception stood the good prince, the son of the king. He stood with majesty amid the white light. Soon all knew that he was the light. The prince once thought to be dead at the hands of the valley people now stood for all to see. He was there. The gates were open. The tomb was unsealed and there he stood. He looked with radiance toward the crowd and the little man and said, "I have paid the price."

The obedient son looked square into the eyes of the odd evil one of deception and corruption and burden and said, "I have paid the price!" The gardener grabbed the corner of his cloak in one hand and tried to shield his eyes and view away from the son.

The crowd stood first in disbelief and then with an increasing knowledge that the son now made everything different. The son once dead, now alive had to make everything different.

Gone from their eyes were the deceiving ploys of the odd little man who for so long had lied to them. They had believed his lies. In a growing remorse, they knew that through his lies and deceptions they had killed the son. The prince had come to relieve their lot in life. They had killed the prince, the son of the king. They began wailing and falling to the ground in realization of their deeds. The tall and the short. The rich and the poor. The mighty and the humble started to fall. They had killed their prince. Unbelief became belief. The distrust that had sprang from the evil one now was exchanged for trust in the risen son. There he was. The prince was there. He had conquered the death so real and final. His power was the power of the king. How or why did they not realize that before they fell upon the prince and caused his death? The folk now understood they had been deceived.

With the coming and rising of the once dead prince, a change came and rose within the townspeople. The crowd in their new belief clearly saw their failure, but the son still paid the price for the valley. The price for them. He had paid it for them. Their evil and willingness for evil so, so clear and evident, but the prince paid the price.

The quaking stopped with the

coming of the risen prince, but a new disturbing din rose around the square. The crowd's voices rose and grew into a roar. It was a victorious shout to honor the prince. The crowd believed.

As one, the crowd turned in their new belief toward the little man. He started to respond that he had been right. He cajoled them with soothing words that once had been so, so effective, but now something was different. Everything now was different. The good obedient son was raised from the tomb. The evil one tried to dissuade the crowd. He tried to convince them that it was he and not the risen prince who was in charge, in control. The crowd knew better. For all of his evil little plans and deceiving little programs, the man knew that now the good prince had won. The king's son had paid the price required. He had purchased everything back unto his father. The little man hung his head and again covered his face with his cloak as if to cover the reality of the truth of the son from his eyes. He moved away from the crowd and tried to retreat from their presence.

As He backed away, he felt something in his pocket. With his other hand, a gnarled corrupted hand he took from the pocket and held the paper he finally was able to find. He was heard telling the crowd, "I have found it! The deed. See I have found it. I am the master of this valley!" His eyes filled with dread and grew to giant proportions as he watched the deed he set such great store by alight with a hot fire and was quickly torched by the flames. He let it go due the pain and the charcoal bits flittered lightly to the ground consumed and useless. His deed proved to be like he was himself. A failure with no value.

The crowd turned on the evil leader and yelled, "Go, get away from us. You lied to us. You deceived us and kept us from the presence of the king and his son. Go! Leave!" The keeper of the gardens in the valley and of the valley itself turned and fled from the anger of the throng. His lies and neglect and burdens and even death had not seen him through to victory. He fled the crowd, then the town and into the valley land. Everyone who saw what happened next was astonished. They viewed the odd man one moment fleeing and in the next moment, before their eyes in an instant vanish. He disappeared and though the valley people could not know where he went, he was gone from the valley land. He vanished into a place where only he could go. A place the king set aside just for him and his sort of evil. The king's prison now was the abode of the odd little gardener. In the face of the victorious son evil must flee.

The prince raised his hands in victory. The crowd no longer living in the stupor of delusion raised their hands both in praise and victory. The son turned from the town's tomb and started to march through the valley land. He sang a triumphal song. The crowd joined the son's song giving glory to the king for sending the son who restored the valley.

They marched by the garden of the burial, but it was no longer a place of mourning. It became a place of life and restoration and resurrection. The most beautiful and majestic flower grew where once was the tomb of the prince. The prince and the valley folk marched by in triumph. Down the path, the throng led by the son marched.

They marched past the garden of the burden where the son had spent the long night. There was no longer a pang of oppression to be felt or displayed. It had become a place of obedience. A place where the son acknowledged his fidelity to the father. A flower, regal and beautiful now grew where once there was a trial. The multitude of valley folk in stride with their leader marched by in both obedience and triumph.

The garden of wilderness no longer was a place of temptation. Temptation had been overcome and was a place of victory. A third brilliant flower grew from the ground where once there was desolation and testing. The multitude marched by in victory and obedience and triumph.

They came to the first garden the son came upon when he entered the valley. The garden of deceit was no longer a place of the lie. It had become a place of the fulfilled promise. The son said he would redeem this garden and he had done that very thing. A fourth flower grew in its beauty where once there was loss. The throng continued past in the glow of the fulfilled promise, victory, obedience and triumph. All of the people of the valley marched and sang and praised the son and the king for saving restoration from the peril and destruction caused by the evil one.

In the entire valley, in the entire kingdom the word would be spread of this day. Everyone spoke of the son's deed and act. An act that cried of the love and mercy of the king's good obedient son. By the son, the rebellion of the valley folk and their once corrupt valley now were brought under the peace and rule of the just king.

## OUR OBEDIENT PRINCE

Our Savior is glorious in that for us, through His passion and sacrifice He has undertaken the remedy making provision on our behalf. He, the Prince is our propitiation and the price for our salvation. We have our all through His grace. He has redeemed us from the evil one. The evil corrupt land where once we lived and the evil nature that once we bore have been conquered by His gift; His death, burial and resurrection, His passion and triumph.

He has for every one of us who believes in Him bought and redeemed us from the garden of deceit. We call it the Garden of Eden. From Adam and Eve's initial fall, we have been held in bondage by the evil one's lie, Genesis chapter 3, but no more.

Our saving Prince has triumphed in the garden of the wilderness. In this garden, the Lord overcame and defeated the evil one's temptations. Our Lord cast aside the offers of bread, the kingdoms and the taunting chides and held fast to the Father's plan, Matthew chapter 4.

Our saving, overcoming and victorious Prince anguished over us in the garden of the burden. We know it as the Garden of Gethsemane, Matthew chapter 26. Our Lord rose from His ordeal in obedience to the Father's will.

Our saving, victorious and obedient Prince finished and accomplished this demonstration of the Father's grace in the garden of the tomb where He lay following His crucifixion. He did not stay there. He arose and in His resurrection, we find the power for our salvation, victory and obedience, Romans chapter 1. Oh, the Savior we serve. A divine Prince, God the Son who would overcome on our behalf in these four gardens all we would and must face in our search for Him. Jesus our Savior, our Prince.

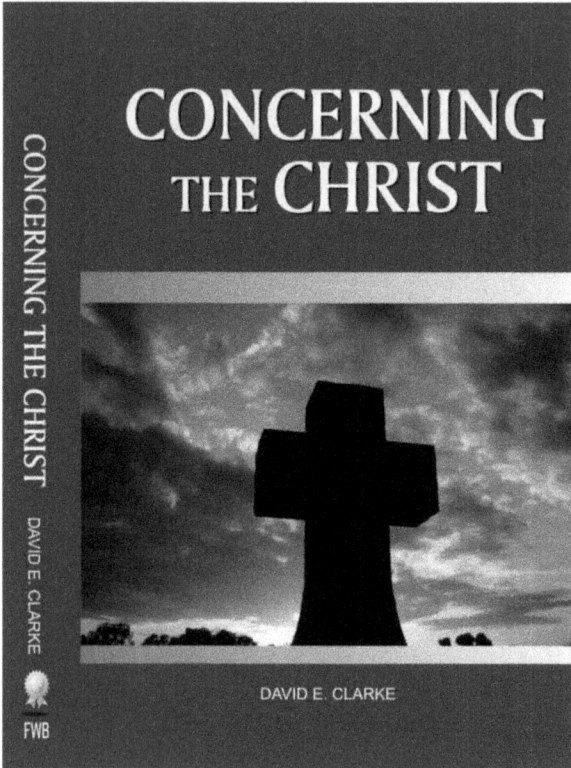

"The Prince and The Four Gardens" was first published within, "Concerning the Christ." FWB Publishing. c. 2011.

*Addition books by David Clarke follows:*

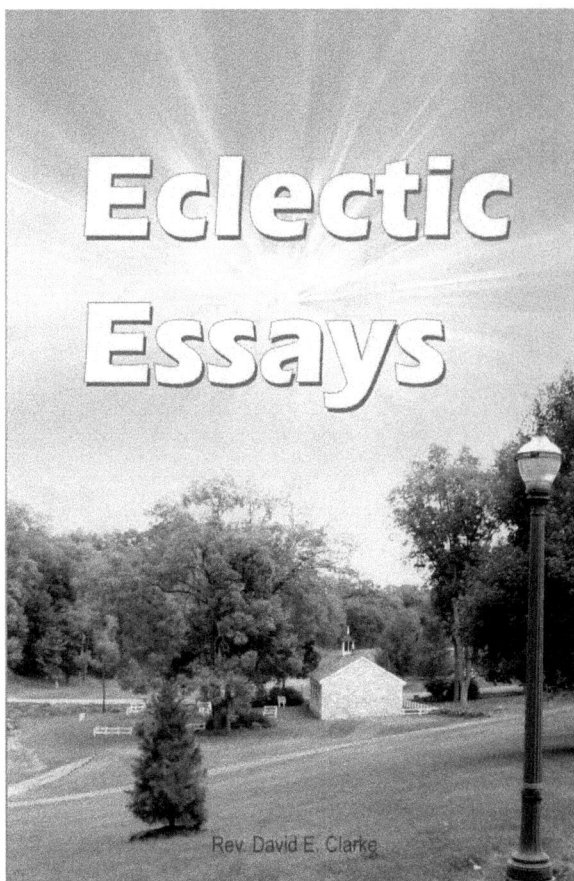

Eclectic Essays

Rev. David E. Clarke

# THE VALLEY WHERE STRANGENESS OCCURS

Rev. David E. Clarke

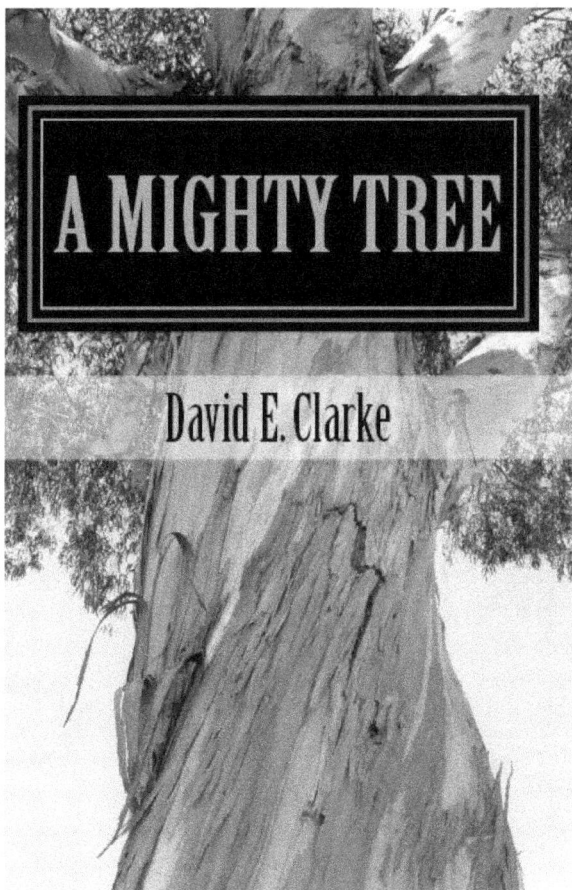

www.ingramcontent.com/pod-product-compliance
Lightning Source LLC
Chambersburg PA
CBHW060610030426
42337CB00018B/3033